'This programme provides a welcome and needed new "po
autism spectrum disorders (ASDs). Attwood and Garnett prov
to help children with ASD experience and express affection and like, something so
important to the human condition and critical to healthy family functioning.'

— *Susan W. White, PhD, Associate Professor, Department of Psychology,*
Director, Psychosocial Interventions Laboratory, Assistant Director, Child
Study Center and Co-Director, Virginia Tech Autism Clinic

affection is a fundamental element for the development and maintenance
nal relationships. The interactive and practical material contained in this
efinitely improve the essential knowledge and fluidity necessary to build
use vanced social skills.'

— *Dr Isabelle Hénault, MA, PhD, psychologist and author of* Asperger's
Syndrome and Sexuality: From Adolescence through Adulthood

'Professo Tony Attwood and Dr Michelle Garnett have created a perfect resource for
home an chool. This easy-to-use book offers great information and guidance. It is
a wonde ul resource that will help children and adolescents understand affection,
enabling hem to build relationships and friendships.'

— *Sue Larkey, autism spectrum specialist, teacher and author of* Making it a Success,
Practical Sensory Programmes *and* Practical Mathematics for Children
with an Autism Spectrum Disorder and Other Developmental Delays

CBT to Help Young People with Asperger's Syndrome (Autism Spectrum Disorder) to Understand and Express Affection

by the same author

The Complete Guide to Asperger's Syndrome
Tony Attwood
ISBN 978 1 84310 495 7 (hardback)
ISBN 978 1 84310 669 2 (paperback)
eISBN 978 1 84642 559 2

Asperger's Syndrome
A Guide for Parents and Professionals
Tony Attwood
Foreword by Lorna Wing
ISBN 978 1 85302 577 8
eISBN 978 1 84642 697 1

Exploring Feelings for Young Children with High-Functioning Autism or Asperger's Disorder
The STAMP Treatment Manual
Angela Scarpa, Anthony Wells and Tony Attwood
ISBN 978 1 84905 920 6
eISBN 978 0 85700 681 3

of related interest

I am Special
A Workbook to Help Children, Teens and Adults with Autism Spectrum Disorders to Understand Their Diagnosis, Gain Confidence and Thrive
2nd edition
Peter Vermeulen
ISBN 978 1 84905 266 5
eISBN 978 0 85700 545 8

CBT to Help Young People with Asperger's Syndrome (Autism Spectrum Disorder) to Understand and Express Affection

A Manual for Professionals

Tony Attwood and Michelle Garnett

Jessica Kingsley *Publishers*
London and Philadelphia

First published in 2013
by Jessica Kingsley Publishers
116 Pentonville Road
London N1 9JB, UK
and
400 Market Street, Suite 400
Philadelphia, PA 19106, USA

www.jkp.com

Library of Congress Cataloging in Publication Data
Attwood, Tony.
  CBT to help young people with Asperger's syndrome (autism spectrum disorder) to understand and express affection : a manual for professionals / Tony Attwood and Michelle Garnett.
    pages cm
  Includes bibliographical references.
  ISBN 978-1-84905-412-6 (alk. paper)
  1. Asperger's syndrome in adolescence--Patients--Life skills guides. 2. Asperger's syndrome in children--Patients--Life skills guides 3. Autistic children--Rehabilitation. 4. Cognitive therapy for teenagers. I. Garnett, Michelle. II. Title. III. Title: Cognitive behavior therapy to help young people with Asperger's syndrome ...
  RJ506.A9A8693 2013
  618.92'858832--dc23
                    2013010989

British Library Cataloguing in Publication Data
A CIP catalogue record for this book is available from the British Library

ISBN 978 1 84905 412 6
eISBN 978 0 85700 801 5

Printed and bound in Great Britain by Bell & Bain Ltd, Glasgow

CONTENTS

PART 1

Introduction

1

WHY CHILDREN AND ADOLESCENTS WHO HAVE ASPERGER'S SYNDROME (AUTISM SPECTRUM DISORDER) NEED A PROGRAMME TO UNDERSTAND AND EXPRESS AFFECTION

Affection in childhood

Within families and friendships, there is an expectation that there is a mutually enjoyable, reciprocal and beneficial regular exchange of words and gestures that express affection. From infancy, children enjoy and seek affection from their parents, and toddlers are able to read the signals when someone expects affection and recognize when to give affection. One of the early signs that clinicians use to diagnose an autism spectrum disorder (ASD) in an infant or child is a lack of appearing to be comforted by affection when distressed. As a typical child matures, there is an intuitive understanding of the type, duration and degree of affection appropriate for the situation and person. Children of under two years know that words and gestures of affection are perhaps the most effective emotional repair mechanism for themselves and for someone who is sad. Unfortunately, for some children with an ASD, a hug can be experienced as an uncomfortable and restricting physical sensation, and the child may soon learn not to cry, as crying will elicit a 'squeeze' from someone. The child with an ASD may also be confused as to why a parent or friend responds to his or her distress with a hug. As an adult with Asperger's syndrome said, 'How does a hug solve the problem?' Sometimes a hug is perceived and enjoyed by a child with an ASD as relaxing deep pressure rather than a gesture to share or alleviate and repair feelings.

From our clinical experience, we have noted that young boys and girls with an ASD may prefer to play with hard toys, such as plastic models of dinosaurs and metal vehicles, rather than soft toys that represent human characteristics and tend to elicit strong feelings and gestures of love and affection in typical children and even adults. Children with an ASD are conspicuous for not sharing when playing with peers. Sharing an activity or toy is perceived by typical children as an indication of their liking for someone, while an aversion to sharing can lead to the perception that they are not being friendly and do not like someone. Children with an ASD may also not recognize the social conventions regarding affection; for example, the child might express and expect in return the same degree of affection with a teacher as they would with their mother. There are also gender differences in the expression of affection between friends, with typical girls anticipating that affection will be integrated within their play. The absence of affection in the play of a girl with an ASD can be a barrier to friendship, and appearing indifferent or aloof to the affection of peers can inhibit social inclusion and contribute to the loss of a potential friendship for both boys and girls.

In general, a child with an ASD may enjoy a very brief and low intensity expression of affection, but become confused or overwhelmed when greater levels of expression are experienced or expected. However, the reverse can occur for some children with an ASD, where they need almost excessive amounts of affection sometimes for reassurance or sensory experience, and often express affection that is too intense or immature. The person with an ASD may not perceive the non-verbal signals and contextual cues in order to know when to stop showing affection, leading to feelings of discomfort or embarrassment in the other person.

When a parent expresses his or her love for an ASD child, perhaps with an affectionate hug, the child's body may stiffen rather than relax to match and fold into the body shape of the parent. The child may also not be soothed by words and gestures of affection when distressed. When an expression of love and affection is rejected or is not effective, parents may wonder what they could do to repair the distress, or whether their son or daughter actually loves or even likes them. The ASD child's rare use of gestures and words of affection can be lamented by parents and friends, who may feel affection-deprived and not demonstrably liked or loved. A mother of a daughter with Asperger's syndrome said that her daughter's lack of affection to family members was 'basically breaking her father's heart, he's devastated'. Another parent said, 'It really hurts that you can't have the relationship you wanted.' If affection is not reciprocated, a parent may try to elicit a greater degree of affection by increasing the intensity and frequency of his or her expressions of affection. This can lead to even greater withdrawal and mutual despair. Another characteristic we have identified from our clinical experience is that of a child with an ASD having a strong attachment to one parent and only accepting and expressing affection with that one parent. This can lead to feelings in the other parent of rejection and jealousy.

When it comes to expressing affection, those with an ASD have a limited vocabulary of actions and gestures, tending to lack subtlety, and (in the case of adolescents) be inappropriate or immature for their age. Their expression of affection and of liking or loving someone may be perceived by family members or friends as too little or too much – drought or flood. An adolescent with Asperger's syndrome explained, 'We feel and show affection, but not often enough, and at the wrong intensity.' Each person has a capacity for expressing and enjoying affection. For a typical person this capacity can be conceptualized as a bucket, but for someone with an ASD, the capacity is a cup that is quickly filled and slow to empty. If the parent fills the affection cup to capacity, the child or adolescent with an ASD can feel saturated with affection and be unable to return the same degree of (or sometimes any) affection.

Affection in adolescence

A teenager with an ASD may not understand the value in an adolescent friendship of mutual exchanges of appreciation and affection that range from liking to loving. Such teenagers may have learned a vocabulary of words and gestures to express affection when very young, and then not modified the actions in recognition of their own maturity and current social conventions. For example, they may invade personal space and not know which parts of someone's body are now inappropriate to touch. The teenager with an ASD may also not know how to progress beyond a reciprocal but platonic friendship, or how to express deeper feelings of affection. There can also be a problem when an adolescent with an ASD develops a 'crush' on a peer. The expression of interest and affection can be perceived as too intense, and the adolescent may not recognize the need for mutual consent or age-appropriate social conventions and boundaries. We use the term 'impaired Theory of Mind' to explain that children and adults who have an ASD are impaired in the ability to conceptualize and reflect on the thoughts and feelings of other people as well as their own thoughts and feelings. Thus, a friend or acquaintance's act of kindness may be misinterpreted as having a more significant meaning than was intended. The person with an ASD may assume that the other person's feelings of affection are reciprocal, and may persistently follow the other person, seeking more acts of kindness. This can result in allegations of stalking and the destruction of the friendship.

Typical adolescents have many friends to provide guidance on the expected and appreciated levels of affection in a friendship or a romantic relationship. Adolescents with an ASD can become increasingly aware of the expressions of affection that occur between their peers and the apparent enjoyment of sensory experiences between a boyfriend and girlfriend. Such relationships can be elusive for a teenager with an ASD, but there may be an intellectual and emotional curiosity and a longing to have similar experiences. The adolescent may seek information and guidance on expressing affection to peers from other sources such as television programmes, which tend to emphasize dramatic expressions of affection; or from pornography on the internet, which portrays age-inappropriate or illegal actions. When such behaviour is suggested or imitated with peers, the adolescent with an ASD can be in serious trouble. Immature and naïve expressions of affection or using a script from a movie or soap opera from a girl who has an ASD can be misinterpreted by those attracted to her as indicating a desire for greater intimacy, which was not her intention. This can lead to accusations of 'leading someone on', and to serious and traumatic experiences.

Another concern for some adolescent males with an ASD is knowing when to stop expressing affection in a romantic relationship. Typical teenagers recognize the verbal and non-verbal signals, the 'amber' or 'red light' signals, that indicate there is no consent to continue. If these signals are not recognized, then there can be accusations of assault and subsequent legal implications.

In their desire to be popular, adolescents with an ASD are vulnerable to being 'set up' by malicious peers. We have known of instances when the person with an ASD has been deliberately misinformed of someone's romantic interest in him or her. When this false assumption leads to unwelcome advances or suggestions, the adolescent is confused, and accused. In contrast, some adolescents who have an ASD are confused by aspects of affection and develop almost a phobia of experiencing, or even seeing, expressions of affection. The person is then perceived as prudish or puritanical.

This programme has been designed primarily for children from 8 to 13 years with an ASD and an intellectual ability within the normal range. However, young children and older adolescents with an ASD who are conspicuously immature may also benefit from the activities and strategies used in the programme. Adults with an ASD may also benefit from aspects of the programme that can be modified to be age-appropriate.

Empathy

A family member or friend could consider that because the person with an ASD rarely expresses affection, especially in situations where affection is anticipated, he or she lacks empathy. Why would such an accusation be made toward someone who may demonstrate many acts of kindness? We know that those with an ASD can be some of the kindest people we have met, for example, a child with an ASD donating all his savings for starving children in Africa. There are two problems that could imply a lack of empathy. The first is the limited ability of the person with an ASD to read subtle body language and contextual cues that indicate someone is feeling distressed. If the subtle signs are not perceived, there will not be the anticipated response of concern, compassion and affection. The second is that the person with an ASD may not know how to respond appropriately, and may fear making a mistake such that it may feel safer to do nothing. In addition, often the first choice for the person with an ASD in such a situation is to repair someone's feelings with a practical act. This can include completing chores, making something or offering help. People who have an ASD can express and enjoy feelings of genuine and deep love and compassion for someone, but usually by practical demonstration rather than words or gestures of affection such as a hug or a kiss. For example, if the distress is due to a damaged or broken object, the first response would be to repair or replace the object. However, if the cause of distress is a broken heart, perhaps because someone has died, the person with an ASD may not know what to do and may be frozen in uncertainty. Thus, the person with an ASD may not recognize that a gesture or words of affection are a quick, powerful and inexpensive emotional restorative for friends and family members.

Affection to repair feelings

We have found that the three most effective emotional repair strategies for someone with an ASD are being alone, being with animals, or engaging in a special interest. This may explain why someone with an ASD may choose to leave alone or avoid his or her parent or friend who is distressed. Another response that can be perceived as uncaring or annoying and indicative of lacking empathy, is to try to engage in a conversation about a special interest. The person is not being callous but actually showing compassion: in other words, if it makes me feel better, it must work for you.

People with an ASD seem able to relate to and express affection and love more easily to animals than people. Thus, parents may observe that the child or adolescent with an ASD can, and often does, express affection for a pet to a level far greater than is expressed for a parent. This can lead to feelings of envy of the pet and resentment that the person can express love but not for a parent. From the ASD perspective, people have complex needs, can deceive or tease you, interrupt and prevent you from engaging in your preferred activities. In contrast, animals are loyal, respectful, predictable and so pleased to see you, and it is easy to make them feel happy. When considering the preferred pets of children and adults who have an ASD, cats are very popular. Tony has sometimes referred to cats as being autistic dogs, hence the ASD person's appreciation of the lifestyle and qualities of cats. Parents may report that their son's or daughter's response to affection is like that of a cat: it is enjoyed sometimes when the child is in a receptive mood, but at other times clearly and almost painfully indicative of discomfort that leads to a parent feeling rejected.

Frequency of affection

We anticipate compliments and frequent words or gestures of affection to confirm and consolidate a relationship or friendship. For the person with an ASD, this can be perceived as repetitive, and the reiteration of the obvious illogical and a waste of time. Once a statement has been made, why should it have to be repeated? A mother complained to her adolescent son that he never said that he loved her. He became very annoyed and replied that he had said he loved her when he was six years old. Why would he need to say it again? Was she developing signs of Alzheimer's?

Sensory sensitivity and affection

It is important that family members and friends recognize a diagnostic aspect of ASD that will affect the ability to enjoy and express affection, and that is hyper- or hypo-reactivity to sensory experiences. For example, some children and adults with an ASD have tactile sensitivity such that light touch on their skin can be perceived as an extremely unpleasant sensory experience. This will obviously affect the enjoyment and response to gestures of affection, such as touching a person's hand or arm during a conversation to emphasize a point or express compassion. Unanticipated touch, due to not reading the signals that this is about to occur (such as a pat on the back or a hug from behind), can elicit a startle response. A kiss can also be perceived as an unpleasant tactile sensation. There may be olfactory sensitivity, such that when experiencing a hug, the person with an ASD can be hyper-aware of someone's perfume or body odour, perceiving it as an extremely unpleasant sensation which is best avoided. All this can explain why some demonstrative family members are avoided.

2

AIMS OF THE PROGRAMME

Psychologists recognize that affection is essential for physical and mental health and an important means of initiating and maintaining friendships and relationships. Although clinicians are rarely asked to help a typical person express liking or love for someone, parents and specialists in autism spectrum disorders are increasingly recognizing that children and adults with an ASD need information and guidance in the understanding and expression of affection.

The aims of the programme are as follows:

1. To help the child discover how expressing and experiencing affection can improve friendships and relationships.

2. To help the child to identify not only his or her own comfort and enjoyment range for gestures, actions and words of affection, but also those of friends and family members.

3. To improve the child's range of expressions for liking and loving someone, appropriate to each relationship and situation.

4. To present explanations which professionals can give to parents and friends regarding the challenges faced by a person with an ASD in reading the signals that indicate when expressions of affection are needed and appreciated.

The programme and manual were originally designed by Professor Tony Attwood and Dr Michelle Garnett, two experienced clinical psychologists in Brisbane, Australia, who have specialized in autism spectrum disorders for several decades. A recent pilot trial of the programme yielded positive results, with children showing increased understanding of the purpose of affection, and parents reporting significant increases in the appropriateness of their children's affectionate behavior (Sofronoff *et al.* 2011). The programme has since been evaluated using a randomized controlled trial and, similarly, the children who took part in the programme showed both increased understanding of affection, and more appropriate use of affection (Andrews, Attwood and Sofronoff, under review).

3

WHO CAN USE THIS PROGRAMME?

This programme, which was designed to be used by teachers, psychologists and therapists, can be conducted with an individual at home or with a group of up to six participants. The activities are fairly simple and there is no requirement for presenters to have particular psychological qualifications or training in psychology before starting the programme. There is an accompanying edition of this book for parents, *From Like to Love for Young People with Asperger's Syndrome (Autism Spectrum Disorder)* (Attwood and Garnett 2013).

4

COGNITIVE BEHAVIOUR THERAPY

The referral of a person with an autism spectrum disorder (ASD), especially Asperger's syndrome, for the psychological treatment of a mood disorder is usually due to concerns regarding the intensity of anxiety, sadness and anger. However, from our extensive clinical experience of children and adolescents with ASD, we would suggest that there is a fourth emotion that is of parental, personal and sometimes clinical concern, namely the ability to understand and express feelings of affection. Children and adolescents with an ASD are often not instinctive and intuitive in expressing their liking or love for someone, or their understanding that family members and friends need regular expressions of affection.

The primary psychological treatment for intense emotions is Cognitive Behaviour Therapy (CBT), which has been developed and refined over several decades. Research studies have established that CBT is an effective treatment to change the way a person thinks about and responds to emotions, especially anxiety, sadness and anger. This is probably the first CBT programme to focus specifically on affection.

CBT focuses on the maturity, complexity, subtlety and vocabulary of emotions, and dysfunctional or illogical thinking and incorrect assumptions. Thus, it has direct applicability to children and adults with an ASD who have impaired or delayed abilities and difficulty understanding, expressing and managing emotions. The theoretical model of emotions used in CBT is consistent with current scientific models of human emotions; namely, becoming more consciously aware of one's emotional state; knowing how to respond to the emotion; becoming more sensitive to how others are feeling; and knowing how to respond to the emotions of others. Knowing how to respond to the emotions of others can be particularly difficult for people with an ASD.

CBT has four components or stages: the first is an assessment of the nature and degree of problems associated with a specific emotion using self-report scales and a clinical interview. The subsequent component is affective education to increase the person's knowledge of emotions. Discussion and activities explore the connection between thoughts, emotions and behaviour, and identify the ways in which the person conceptualizes emotions and perceives various situations. The more someone understands emotions, the more he or she is able to express and control them appropriately. The third stage of CBT is cognitive restructuring to correct distorted conceptualizations and dysfunctional beliefs and to constructively manage emotions. The last stage is a schedule of activities for practising new cognitive skills to comprehend and express emotions in real life situations. All of these components are included in this programme.

CBT includes education in when and how to express emotions, the appropriate intensity for the person and the situation, and with what frequency. We have applied the strategies used in CBT, such as affective education, to help the person with an ASD understand the concept and feelings of affection in themselves and others; cognitive restructuring to change thinking and behaviour; and desensitization to reduce the anxiety, confusion and frustration often associated with feelings of affection. The intention is gradually to increase the person's tolerance and enjoyment of affection, as well as his or her ability and confidence in expressing affection, ranging from like to love in a friendship or within the family. Once the person with ASD learns to enjoy affection, they are able to accept the reassurance that is inherent in affectionate acts: that they are personally likeable and lovable.

The person with ASD, despite feeling confused about affection and its expression, still has the very human need for approval, liking and love. Thus, as the new skills of affection are practised, they become self-reinforcing. Becoming open to the feedback that they are liked and loved by friends and family leads that person to feel greater self-acceptance and self-confidence in social situations. Greater engagement in friendships and family becomes possible, and provides important preparation for future relationships.

We now have published case studies and objective scientific evidence that CBT does significantly reduce problems in the communication and expression of emotions in children and adults with an ASD. A clinical psychologist usually implements a CBT programme, but this programme was designed to be implemented by teachers as well as by psychologists (educational or clinical), psychiatrists, speech and language pathologists/therapists or occupational therapists.

The neurology of affection

Research using neuro-imaging technology with people who have an ASD has identified structural and functional abnormalities of the amygdala, a part of the brain associated with the recognition and regulation of emotions. The amygdala is known to regulate a range of emotions including anger, anxiety, sadness and affection. Thus, we also have neuro-anatomical evidence that suggests there will be problems with the perception and regulation of emotions, such as affection, for those who have an ASD.

Temple Grandin explained that:

> My brain scan shows that some emotional circuits between the frontal cortex and the amygdala just aren't hooked up – circuits that affect my emotions and are tied to my ability to feel love. I experience the emotion of love, but it's not the same way that most neurotypical people do. Does this mean my love is less valuable than what other people feel? (Grandin and Barron 2005, p.40)

PART 2

How to Conduct the Programme

5

ASSESSMENT OF THE ABILITY TO COMMUNICATE AFFECTION

Questionnaires

When the original CBT programme for affection was being designed, there were no standardized measures of affection that could be applied to children and adolescents who have an ASD. Drs Sofronoff, Lee and Sheffield, and Tony from the University of Queensland, Australia, developed and evaluated three measures of affection that could be used to explore the ability of typical children and adolescents, and those with an ASD, to communicate affection and to measure any changes attributable to a CBT programme (Sofronoff *et al.*, in press). The three questionnaires, which are in Appendix 2 of this book, are described below.

The Affection for Others Questionnaire (AOQ)

The AOQ is a 20-item questionnaire that examines giving and receiving verbal and physical affection, and the communication of empathy by the child, to *classmates*, *friends* and *family members*. The AOQ was designed with five subscales: Giving Verbal Affection to Others, Giving Physical Affection to Others, Receiving Verbal Affection from Others, Receiving Physical Affection from Others, and Communicating Empathy to Others. Each of these subscales was found to have good internal consistency, with Cronbach's alpha coefficients for each subscale ranging from .85 to .94 (Sofronoff *et al.* 2011). There are four questions within each subscale, making a total of 20 questions. There are two parts to each question. The first part asks parents about the appropriateness of the child's affectionate gestures. Scores range from 1, 'Never appropriate', through to 7, 'Always appropriate'. The second part of the question assesses the amount of affection that their child displays, with responses ranging from 1, 'Not enough', to 7, 'Too much'.

To score the AOQ, sum the appropriateness and amount scores separately for each of the following scales: Communicating Empathy to Others, Giving Affection to Others, and Receiving Affection from Others. (Giving Affection to Others combines the Giving Verbal Affection to Others and Giving Physical Affection to Others subscales. Receiving Affection from Others combines the Receiving Verbal Affection from Others and Receiving Physical Affection from Others subscales.) A Total Appropriateness score and a Total Amount of Affection score is calculated by adding the totals for each subscale. In all, 10 scores are possible.

The questionnaire was given to 54 children with Asperger's syndrome who participated in a randomized controlled trial of the affection programme (Andrews, Attwood and Sofronoff, under review). Means and standard deviations for the AOQ Total Appropriateness, Giving Affection to Others, Receiving Affection from Others, and Communicating Empathy to Others scales across two time points are given in the table below. Time 1 refers to questionnaire administration at the start of the Affection programme, and Time 2 refers to questionnaire administration at the completion of the Affection programme. For full details of the RCT please refer to the original article (Andrews, Attwood and Sofronoff, under review).

Means and standard deviations of AOQ subscale scores across time (N = 54)

Measure	Time 1		Time 2	
	M	SD	M	SD
AOQ – Total Appropriateness	65.61	(19.32)	79.70	(16.76)
AOQ – Giving Affection	26.22	(8.89)	31.22	(7.55)
AOQ – Receiving Affection	28.50	(9.40)	32.30	(7.60)
AOQ – Communicating Empathy	14.30	(4.18)	16.19	(3.48)

To interpret the Total Amount of Affection score: scores 59 and below are considered 'Low affection', scores between 59 and 100 are considered 'Adequate affection', and scores 101 and above are considered 'High affection'. Means are not provided for this score because the way parents rate the affectionate behaviour of their child is not linear; that is, improvements to the child's appropriate use of affection can be demonstrated by both increases and decreases on this scale. A desired outcome is that the child is demonstrating 'Adequate affection'.

The Affection for You Questionnaire (AYQ)

The AYQ is a 19-item questionnaire that examines giving and receiving verbal and physical affection, and the communication of empathy by the child, to a *parent*.

Similar to the AOQ, there are five subscales within the AYQ, and each of these was found to have good internal consistency with Cronbach's alpha coefficients between .9 and .95 (Sofronoff *et al.* 2011). There are two parts to each question. The first part of the question measures the frequency of affection shown to the parent, on a scale from 1, 'Never', to 7, 'Twice a day or more'. This part of the questionnaire is a qualitative measure and no score is calculated.

The second part of the question measures the amount of affection, Total Affection, on a scale from 1, 'Not enough', to 7, 'Too much'. To calculate the Total Affection score, simply sum all of the circled numbers for the second part of each question in the questionnaire.

To interpret these scores: a score of 57 and below is considered 'Low affection', a score between 57 and 95 is denoted as 'Adequate affection', and a score of 96 or over is categorized as 'High affection'. As for the AOQ above, a desired outcome is that the child shows 'Adequate affection'.

The General Affection Questionnaire (GAQ)

The GAQ is a 12-item questionnaire that examines aspects of affectionate communication such as expressing inadequate or excessive affection, the importance of affection in the person's daily life, and the degree to which teaching and support regarding affection are required. To complete the questionnaire, the parent assigns a rating from 1, 'Strongly disagree', to 7, 'Strongly agree' to each of 12 statements. These statements variously assess the amount of affection the child shows, the appropriateness of that affection, the impact of the difficulties with affection the child has, and the child's knowledge of affection. To score, simply sum all of the 12 items to give a Total Difficulty with Affection score.

In the RCT study (Andrews *et al.*, under review), the mean score for 54 children with Asperger's syndrome was 42.19, and the standard deviation was 14.9. The GAQ was not found to be a sensitive measure of change across the time of the Affection programme, and may be more useful in the initial assessment to determine where the child's difficulties lie.

Stories

After listening to each of the stories described below, which can be found in Appendix 1, the child or adolescent is asked certain questions that relate to the communication of affection. The stories can help to assess the child's understanding of the purpose of affection. Read each scenario to the child and record the child's responses. The score for each story is obtained by allocating one point for each appropriate response. The 'A Walk in the Forest' test has been found to be a sensitive measure of change in the understanding of affection (Sofronoff *et al.* 2011).

A Walk in the Forest

The main theme of this story is to imagine meeting an alien who has recently landed on planet Earth, and explaining to the alien why humans are affectionate to each other. This can elicit the child's depth of understanding of the value of affection.

Returning Home from School

The child is asked to imagine returning from school to find Mum sitting at the kitchen table in tears, and evidently in great distress. It is explained that her distress has nothing to do with the child, who is then asked what he or she would do in that situation. A first response is usually to ask, 'What is the matter?' or, 'What has happened?' Then, more importantly, the child is asked what he or she would do or say to make Mum feel better. The answers are analyzed to indicate whether affection is expressed and how, the type of affection (such as giving a hug), and whether there is a greater emphasis on practical means of emotion recovery, such as offering to do the washing up or handing Mum a tissue.

A Friend Feeling Sad

The child is asked to imagine arriving at school just before his or her friend. The friend enters the school grounds looking very sad, and explains that early that morning his or her dog escaped from home, ran across a road, was hit by a car, and died. The child is asked what he or she would do in that situation to console the friend.

Pre- and post-programme assessment

The three affection questionnaires and the three stories can be administered just before participating in the programme to provide useful information for the adult conducting or presenting the programme. It is important to know the participant's affection communication profile from the questionnaires, and understand the conceptualization of affection, and type of affection used in specific situations, from the three stories. The questionnaires and stories can also be administered after the final session of the programme to measure any cognitive and behavioural changes.

6

How to run group and individual sessions

Children and adolescents with an ASD are more responsive to programmes that are highly structured and appeal to the logical or scientific thinking associated with ASD. Their cognitive profile can include remarkable visual reasoning abilities such that activities are enhanced with the use of pictures and drawing, thereby placing less emphasis on conversation. Due to problems with generalization and the recall of information in different situations associated with ASD, role plays and practice in real-life situations need to be included in the programme to a greater extent than would occur with a typical child. It is also important that the professional conducting the programme has an understanding of other characteristics of people with an ASD, for example, the tendency to make literal interpretations such that idioms and metaphor could be confusing. If running the programme within a group format, the ratio of presenter to participants will vary from a ratio of one to two to one to four, depending on the degree of experience of the clinician.

The approach used in this programme is to appeal to the logical thinking of children and adolescents with an ASD. Due to their problems with Theory of Mind, compared to typical children, there needs to be a greater component of the programme devoted to how to discover the salient cues that indicate specific thoughts and feelings, and how to perceive the various levels of affection from like to love within themselves and others. Strategies specifically designed for children with an ASD to improve Theory of Mind abilities are Social Stories™ and Comic Strip Conversations™, which have been developed by Carol Gray (see Recommended Resources). Social Stories™ enable adults to explore and understand the perspective of the ASD child or adolescent, discover together how the child can express an appropriate level of affection in a specific situation, and explain the value of expressing affection. For example, Social Stories™ can be used to explain why friends and family need frequent reminders that they are liked or loved, even if they have no reason to doubt there is genuine affection for that friend or family member. Comic Strip Conversations™ use simple drawings with stick figures, and thought, speech and emotion bubbles to illustrate events and emotions. They are particularly useful in correcting inaccurate or dysfunctional perceptions of social situations and emotions. A parent may create a Social Story™ or use Comic Strip Conversations™ during a session to supplement the designated activity within the session.

While research on Theory of Mind abilities have identified the problems children and adolescents with an ASD have in 'reading' emotional states, clinical experience and research have also confirmed characteristics of alexithymia, namely, a diminished vocabulary to describe the different levels of emotional experience, especially for the more subtle or complex emotions. The affective education component of CBT is also important in improving the vocabulary of the child or adolescent with an ASD to describe emotions, thereby diminishing the effects of alexithymia. The approach adopted in this programme is to quantify the degree of expression such that if the precise word was elusive, the child could calibrate and express his or her degree of liking or loving someone using a thermometer or numerical rating, thus indicating the intensity of experience and enjoyment.

The programme includes worksheets for the child to record information (see Part 3), although this aspect is deliberately kept to a minimum since children with an ASD often have poor handwriting skills and prefer to listen, watch and do, rather than write. If there is a genuine aversion to writing, the professional conducting the programme can listen to the participant's spoken comments and answers and write them on the worksheets. Readers have permission to photocopy all worksheets marked with a ✓ for personal use. They are also available to download from www.jkp.com/catalogue/book/9781849054126/resources.

At the end of each session the project to be completed before the next session is explained, and the information obtained from the project discussed at the start of the subsequent session. The project was designed to obtain more information or data and to apply strategies in real situations. Children with an ASD often have an aversion to the concept of homework from bitter school experiences, so the professional conducting the programme needs to emphasize the importance of completing the project, and clearly encourage the child to do so. There will also need to be good collaboration between home and school with regard to expressing affection to friends. It is important that teachers are aware of the programme, and ways in which they can contribute to the child's knowledge base on expressing and responding to affection with peers. They can also help with the successful implementation of strategies.

The general approach is to emphasize success and discovery, acknowledging contributions and discouraging 'right' or 'wrong' answers. Positive suggestions from the child are always encouraged. The professional presenters of the programme such as a teacher, psychologist or therapist can deviate from the prescribed text to accommodate the individual, and use aspects of ASD to illustrate a point, for example, the feelings of elation associated with a special interest as a metaphor for feeling love for someone. The duration of each activity is variable, according to the attention and learning capacity and rate of progress of the child, however, as a general guide, each session is designed to be covered within one hour. The activities do not have to be completed in the sequence they occur in the workbook, and a parent or presenters may include additional activities and resources. Thus, the programme is flexible in structure and duration, and can evolve to meet the needs of different individuals.

Group sessions

If the programme is being conducted using a group format by a teacher or psychologist, there may need to be careful selection of group participants. We recognize that children and adolescents with an ASD are at risk of additional diagnoses, particularly ADHD and oppositional defiant disorder. A dual diagnosis will impact on the cohesion of the group. It is also important to consider the personality of each participant and his or her emotional and intellectual maturity in order to maximize group cooperation, mutual support and the possibility of the development of friendships within and after the group sessions. If a group format is used, we recommend that the ratio of presenter to participants should vary from a ratio of one to two to one to four, depending on the degree of experience of the clinician, in order to most effectively monitor and facilitate group interactions and attention.

Achieving group cohesion

It is important to select participants in a way that reduces the potential for personality clashes and ensures an even distribution of support needs. Having several participants who require extra supervision and explanations in comparison to other group members can affect the rate of progress and group cohesion. The ratio of presenter to participants is much easier if it is one to two, as the content of the programme requires the presenters to carefully observe the degree of engagement and comprehension of the participants. One presenter can lead each activity, while the other presenter maintains attention and records information.

There must also be some consideration of the venue for the programme when conducted using a group format, with the provision of sufficient personal space and comfortable chairs, and an awareness of the sensory issues associated with ASD, for example, olfactory and tactile sensitivity, and sensitivity to bright light and the sound of machinery. It is also important that the person conducting the programme is aware of the time children with an ASD take to process and respond to social/emotional information, and that such children are very sensitive to emotional atmosphere and attitude, especially criticism and negativity.

Clinical experience has identified that children with an ASD are prone to developing an almost pathological fear of failure, errors or making a mistake. To accommodate and counter this fear of failure there needs to be an emphasis throughout the programme on encouraging self-confidence, explaining that not knowing or making an error is not a disaster but an opportunity to learn and become wiser. It is important to positively reinforce the child's abilities throughout the programme.

At the start of the programme the presenters should introduce themselves and each participant to the group. There will need to be agreed ground rules on potential issues such as taking turns to speak, keeping to the point, and being courteous and friendly. The presenters will also need to ensure there are sufficient pencils and erasers for all the participants.

We have found that during the group sessions, a child may show remarkable moments of insight or clarity of expression. We call these 'Words of Wisdom'. There may also be moments of humour. During each group session, one of the presenters records the key points discovered by the participants, along with any 'Words of Wisdom' or humorous comments. These are printed and distributed to the participants at the start of the next session.

Time with parents after each group session

The programme should include time at the end of each session with the participants' parents, usually 30 minutes in group format. The aim of the sessions are to exchange information regarding their son's or daughter's responses and abilities during the activities, and to explain the project and seek information on particular issues that could be addressed in a subsequent session. It is also essential that family members are encouraged to respond positively and appropriately to the participants' new abilities and understanding of affection, and to facilitate the successful application of strategies discovered during the programme in real life situations. Clinical experience of the programme has indicated that some family members of a person with an ASD may also have problems communicating affection, and group discussion with parents may encourage solutions to problems experienced by other family members.

During the first session we ask each parent to briefly introduce their son or daughter by way of age and personality characteristics, and to state their most important goal for the group. The sharing of problems/goals in this way can be a quick way to assist the parents to feel less alone, as they quickly discover that their problems are not unique. It is important during this activity that one group facilitator take careful notes. During the first or second session, a suggestion is made to exchange email addresses with each other for communication beyond the group. The format of subsequent sessions with the parents essentially follows each workbook, sharing both the information given out to the children and unique information about each child during the group. The last five minutes of each session is dedicated to sharing the project for the week and encouraging parents to assist their child to complete their project.

7

SESSION COMPONENTS

Below we summarize the component activities for each session. Over the next chapters we then describe the sessions in more detail.

Session 1: Introduction to the programme – Exploring feelings of affection

Initial assessment through stories (from Appendix 1).

1. The activities and experiences that you like.

2. People whom you like or love.

3. How do those people express that they like you or love you?

4. How we feel, think and behave when someone likes or loves us.

5. What would life be like without being liked or loved?

6. List some of the things that are not so nice about being liked or loved.

7. Project: Collect pictures of people expressing affection.

8. Project: Family affection.

9. Project: Social Story™.

Session 2: Beginning to recognize and express affection

Review of Session 1.

1. A Social Story™ about how liking or loving someone can affect your feelings, thoughts and abilities.

2. Using the like and love thermometer to explore pictures of liking and loving.

3. What can you say and do to show that you like someone?

4. What can you say and do to show that you love someone?

5. Project: Use the ideas at home to express liking or loving a member of the family.

Session 3: Giving and receiving compliments

Review of Session 2.

1. Review the project from Session 2.

2. Why do we give compliments?

3. Compliments for specific people.

4. Types of compliment.

5. How often should you give someone a compliment?

6. How do you reply to a compliment?

7. Practise giving and receiving compliments.

8. Could a compliment be embarrassing?

9. Project: Create a compliment diary.

Session 4: The reasons we express like or love through affectionate words and gestures

Review of Session 3.

1. Review the compliment diary project from Session 3.

2. Why do we give affection?

3. What would happen if nobody showed you that they liked or loved you?

4. What would happen if you stopped showing your friends that you liked them?

5. If you did not get enough affection, how could you make yourself feel better?

6. How do you feel when…?

7. Project: Complete a diary of receiving and giving affection.

Session 5: Developing our skills at expressing affection

Review of Session 4.

1. Review the diary of receiving and giving affection from Session 4.

2. Different types of affection in different situations.

3. How can you tell if someone needs affection?

4. How can you tell if you have given *too much* affection?

5. How can you tell if you have given *not enough* affection?

6. What are the three most important things you have learned about affection?

7. Complete the post-programme assessments.

8. Express affection to someone in the group with a compliment or gesture such as a hug.

9. Receive your certificate of knowledge!

SESSION OVERVIEWS

Session 1: Introduction to the programme – Exploring feelings of affection

Initial assessment through stories

The affection questionnaires from Appendix 2 should have been completed by parents in advance of the session, and the other affection assessment measures (the three stories from Appendix 1) completed by the child or each participant also prior to the first session. This information is invaluable in determining specific issues to be addressed during the programme for each participant. The information from the assessments should have been reviewed and discussed by the presenters before the first session. For this first session, the presenters will need to distribute large sheets of paper for each child to draw thermometers, and small 'Post Its' to record specific activities, experiences or names.

If a group format is used, it is important to ensure that the room is large enough for the number of participants and types of activity. There should be a white board or large sheets of paper on a wall to record important ideas and words of wisdom from the participants. This information is typed in a document that is distributed to all participants and reviewed at the next session.

The session starts with an introduction of presenters and participants, and distribution of the workbook, pencils, erasers and other materials.

Ground rules are established and agreed. The ground rules are distributed to each participant at the next session.

1. The activities and experiences that you like

The aim is to identify up to ten activities or experiences that the child likes and to measure the degree of enjoyment on a scale of 0–100. The activity introduces the concept of a thermometer to measure the degree of feeling. Group discussion or discussion with a parent can explore how the same experience can be rated very similarly or very differently by different people. When the special interest is one of the activities or experiences, it is important to explore the range of positive feeling associated with the interest. To get things started, the presenters can nominate some activities that are known to be enjoyed, such as being alone, achieving a perfect score in a test or not having any homework.

2. People whom you like or love

This is a similar activity, but this time the child identifies ten people that he or she likes or loves. These people can be family members, friends or real life or fictional heroes. On the thermometer, 0 to 50 measures the depth of liking someone, while 51 to 100 measures the depth of love. Discussion can focus on individual differences in the degree of liking and loving specific people and why. The presenters may need to ensure that the child's ten people illustrate different levels on the thermometer. Children with an ASD may need guidance in recognizing that liking and loving is not an 'either/or' dichotomy, and that people they like or love are not all exclusively within a narrow range of appreciation. There may be some debate as to whether to include a pet in the list. Experience with children with an ASD has shown that it can be interesting to explore the degree of affection associated with a pet in comparison to a person.

3. How do those people express that they like you or love you?

For typical children this can be an easy activity, but children with an ASD often have difficulty spontaneously identifying the ways people show how much he or she is liked or loved. The examples should be from both family members and friends, in order to facilitate initial discussion of the different ways of expressing affection in a friendship compared to within a family. The first stage is to elicit spontaneous examples. Following this, the presenters nominate suggestions to evaluate whether the child actually does or could recognize a wider range of expressions. This activity can also be discussed at the subsequent meeting with other family members to explore which expressions have not been perceived or recorded by the child. We have found that children with an ASD often prioritize and notice practical expressions of affection such as buying a present or playing a game of their choice, yet fail to recognize words or gestures of affection, such as a hug, or being told that the family member loves them. It may also be important to discover and define any idiosyncratic words for affection used within the family.

4. How we feel, think and behave when someone likes or loves us

This activity explores how affection can positively affect feelings, thinking and abilities. The information from this and the subsequent activity will be used in the creation of a Social Story™ that will be discussed at the next session. In a group format, this is an activity primarily conducted as a discussion involving all group members. Some important aspects of affection can be explored, such as how affection can help someone relax when anxious; re-energize, build confidence and infuse optimism when someone is sad; and act as a quick, easy and cheap emotional restorative for friends and family members.

5. What would life be like without being liked or loved?

The discussion focuses on how an absence or lack of affection could lead to the opposite of the thoughts and feelings described in activity number 4. For example, feeling anxious, lacking energy, having low confidence and feeling pessimistic and sad.

6. List some of the things that are not so nice about being liked or loved

This activity explores some of the not-so-nice aspects of being liked or loved. This can include being vulnerable to being disappointed, feeling sad when someone is not there, and the need for solitude if a friend expects to accompany you more than is comfortable, or expects you to be part of a larger group. There can also be concerns about sensory sensitivity, worrying about someone, and grief, should a relative (such as a grandparent) die.

7. Project: Collect pictures of people expressing affection

The child is asked to collect pictures of people expressing affection. These pictures are to be used in an activity in Session 2. Source material for pictures can be magazines for women and families, for adolescents gossip magazines or internet clip art. Copies of family photographs where family members are expressing affection can also be included in the project.

8. Project: Family affection

The child is asked to identify situations where affection is expected, but that he or she finds difficult. The main focus is on situations within the family, but the presenters may decide that the project can also include situations with friends. This is an activity to be completed by the child with a parent, with the primary focus being on close family members. However, the activity can be extended to a wider family circle, and significant adults in the child's life, such as a teacher and friends or classmates. The information will be used in a subsequent activity.

9. Project: Social Story™

Between sessions, the presenters will need to write a Social Story™ using material elicited during activities 4 and 5 from Session 1. Social Stories™ were originally developed by Carol Gray (see Recommended Resources). A Social Story™ describes a situation, skill or concept in terms of relevant social cues, perspectives and common responses in a specifically defined style and format. The intention is to share accurate social and emotional information in a reassuring and informative manner that is easily understood by the child with Asperger's syndrome. Carol Gray has developed a Social Story™ formula such that the text describes more than directs with more information available from www.thegraycenter.org.

In a group format, the meeting immediately after the session with parents provides an opportunity to discuss individual participants and their responses to each activity, and to validate specific comments. It will be necessary to stress the importance of completing the project each week, as this provides valuable information and the opportunity to improve the communication of affection in real situations.

Session 2: Beginning to recognize and express affection

Review of Session 1

After reviewing the ground rules, the second session starts with a revision of the key points and words of wisdom from the last session, which are distributed in written form to the participants or an individual child. A quick quiz is used to enable the child to recall someone who is liked or loved and how much, using the scale or thermometer from 0 to 100.

1. A Social Story™ about how liking or loving someone can affect your feelings, thoughts and abilities

The presenters of the programme then read aloud the Social Story™ or stories using the suggestions from the participants or the individual child in the previous session on how liking or loving someone can affect feelings, thoughts and behaviour.

2. Using the like and love thermometer to explore pictures of liking and loving

The first part of the project was to collect pictures or photographs that illustrate different levels of liking or loving someone. Draw a thermometer on a very large piece of paper on the floor. The child or participants place each of his or her pictures at the appropriate point on the thermometer. There may need to be guidance and discussion if there are areas of disagreement or an unusual rating of the degree of affection. It is also important to accommodate and explain various cultural and family differences.

Part of this activity can be to learn the words and facial expressions that describe different levels of affection, from 'concerned' to 'loving'. *The Cognitive Affective Training kit or CAT-kit* (see Recommended Resources) can be used as an additional resource to improve the participants' vocabulary to describe different levels of affection.

3. What can you say and do to show that you like someone?

For this activity in a group format, the participants separate into pairs. With an individual child, the pair is child and parent. One of the pair creates a list of actions or statements that you can do or say to show that you like someone. He or she also rates, from 1 to 50, the degree of liking that each action or statement indicates. In a group format, the other person records the responses and ratings. When the list has at least five examples, the roles are reversed.

When the lists are completed, there is discussion of the actions and statements, providing the child with an opportunity to learn new expressions of liking someone.

An additional activity can be to explore how animals, and especially pets, express liking someone.

4. What can you say and do to show that you love someone?

The format is the same as in the previous activity, this time for love, with a rating from 51 to 100.

The presenters may discuss the different degree of affection expressed by specific actions, and variations in the quality, intensity and duration of an action. For example, the child may have a limited 'vocabulary' of hugs – one size fits all. There can be role play activities to discover different types of hug, perhaps with a numerical value from 1 to 10 that reflect the degree of affection being expressed and exchanged. There may also need to be information on the different types of kiss, from greeting a distant family member to expressing love to a parent. The *Cognitive Affective Training kit* or *CAT-kit* (see Recommended Resources) includes a silhouette of a body, and this resource can be used to illustrate where on the body is an appropriate place to kiss according to cultural and family conventions.

Feedback from Session 1 project for a group format

In turn, the participants share with the group their findings from the Session 1 project. They each describe a situation where affection is anticipated with a particular family member. Together, they make suggestions as to when affection should be expressed in the particular situation described, and to what degree. The participants record these suggestions on their handouts.

5. Project: Use the ideas at home to express liking or loving a member of the family

The project between Sessions 2 and 3 is for the child to actually express affection for the nominated family member, using the ideas discussed in Session 2, and to discuss at the next session what he or she did or said, what the reaction of the family member was and how the family member felt. The project could also be extended to include expressions of affection for significant adults or friends and classmates.

Session 3: Giving and receiving compliments

Review of Session 2

The third session starts with a reminder of what happened in the previous session. Key points and words of wisdom are discussed and refreshed.

1. Review the project from Session 2

Discussion of the project is the first activity, and the child discloses and shares situations within the family (or friendship) where there is an expectation of affection. The child provides feedback on who was the recipient, the type of affection, the response of the other person and how he or she felt when expressing affection. The presenters emphasize the positive consequences for both the person receiving and the person giving affection.

The main theme for Session 3 is giving and receiving compliments.

2. Why do we give compliments?

This is an activity exploring the thoughts and feelings that someone is expressing when giving a family member or friend a compliment. The presenters explain that compliments can be divided into five categories of thoughts or feelings:

- admiration
- reassurance
- friendship
- encouragement
- liking or loving someone.

3. Compliments for specific people

In the first activity, the child suggests a compliment for a friend for each of the five categories of thoughts or feelings described above. The child can then create a compliment for specific family members for four of the same five categories (in this instance, 'friendship' is not needed).

4. Types of compliment

The child may need guidance regarding what qualities in a person can be appropriately acknowledged by a compliment. This activity is designed to explore the different types of compliment that can be expressed about someone's abilities, appearance and personality. The child creates a compliment for a friend or family member based on these attributes.

5. How often should you give someone a compliment?

As described in the introduction to this programme, children, and often adults, with an ASD may not express affection as often as would be expected and appreciated by a friend or family member. Giving someone a compliment can be an expression of affection. The presenters will need to explain that compliments should not be a rare expression of liking or loving someone and should probably be expressed to a friend or family member on a more frequent basis.

6. How do you reply to a compliment?

This activity is designed to provide guidance and discussion on how to respond to a compliment. The two main anticipated responses are to express appreciation and agreement. The child creates examples of how to express appreciation and agreement.

7. Practise giving and receiving compliments

The next activity is to work in pairs, if a group format is being used or the parent and child together, and to practise giving and responding to compliments and to explore and share the feelings of the person giving and the person receiving the compliment. This can be a very enjoyable activity.

8. Could a compliment be embarrassing?

Children with an ASD may not be as aware as typical peers of social conventions when giving a compliment, or as able to perceive and appreciate that the compliment he or she is giving may be true, but could be embarrassing for the recipient. This activity explores the types of compliment that could be embarrassing for a classmate, friend or family member. The presenters will need to encourage discussion and understanding of why some compliments could be perceived as embarrassing, and how to recognize the signals. This activity is particularly important for teenagers seeking a relationship beyond friendship. Role plays and the use of specific resources, such as the interactive DVD *Mind Reading: The Interactive Guide to Emotions* (see Recommended Resources) can help the child identify the verbal and non-verbal signs of embarrassment.

9. Project: Create a compliment diary

The project between sessions is for the child to keep a diary of compliments that he or she receives and gives each day.

Session 4: The reasons we express like or love through affectionate words and gestures

Review of Session 3

Session 4 begins in the usual way, with the distribution of the key points and words of wisdom from Session 3.

1. Review the compliment diary project from Session 3

This is followed by a brief review of compliments and the compliment diary, with discussion of the feelings of the person giving and receiving the compliment, and any subsequent effects on the friendship or relationship.

2. Why do we give affection?

Now that the expression of affection has been explored over three sessions, the child, first as an individual then, if a group format is being used, as a group, suggests reasons why people give each other affection. Some of the answers will already have been generated early in Session 1, but at this stage in the programme, there will be more reasons identified and appreciated. There can be a comparison between the two lists and what has been learned and appreciated.

3. What would happen if nobody showed you that they liked or loved you?

This activity explores how the child would feel if he or she did not experience demonstrations of being liked or loved.

These responses can lead into the next activity and be used to illustrate how a friend or relative would feel if expressions of affection were not made by the participant to that person.

4. What would happen if you stopped showing your friends that you liked them?

This activity further explores the theme of feeling bereft of affection, primarily for a friend, but the discussion can progress to how a family member would feel. The activity also includes strategies to repair the feelings of a friend (or family member) associated with not experiencing expressions of affection.

5. If you did not get enough affection, how could you make yourself feel better?

This activity is for the child who may feel that he or she does not experience enough affection. Sometimes a parent of a child with an ASD may also have a problem expressing affection and this activity can explore strategies to cope, cheer oneself up and achieve compensatory affection from someone else, or a pet. In a group format, this activity can be an important point of discussion within the parents' meeting after this session.

6. How do you feel when...?

A questionnaire is used to explore the child's depth of enjoyment or discomfort experienced in response to specific expressions of affection. Experience has indicated a wide range of individual responses that can be discussed.

7. Project: Complete a diary of receiving and giving affection

The child completes a diary for six very specific expressions of affection. The intention is to actively encourage expressing each type of affection at least twice a day, and to record an example of these expressions of affection. Parents will need to actively support the child to complete the log book each day.

Session 5: Developing our skills at expressing affection

Review of Session 4

After a brief review of the key points and words of wisdom, Session 4 starts with recalling the feelings associated with experiencing affection. There is discussion about the consequences for the child if he or she did not express affection to a friend or family member.

1. Review the diary of receiving and giving affection from Session 4

This is followed by a review, sharing and discussion of the information and experiences recorded in the diary of receiving and giving affection.

2. Different types of affection in different situations

This activity is a game to match specific types of affection to a particular situation. There are appropriate matches, but there can also be some fun making inappropriate matches, and exploring why they are inappropriate, for example, saying to the postman, 'I love you', or giving your mum a handshake when she is crying.

3. How can you tell if someone needs affection?

This activity can be very difficult for children with an ASD, especially with regard to identifying subtle signals. Additional activities and resources could be used, for example the presenters role playing (and replaying on video) someone who is expressing subtle signs of distress and asking the child which non-verbal cues indicated a need for affection and what would be an appropriate response if that person was a friend or family member. Short video clips and audio recordings from *Mind Reading: The Interactive Guide to Emotions* (see Recommended Resources) can be used to supplement and extend the activity if needed.

In a group format, the child can work in pairs and use role play to practise expressing and recognizing the subtle signals of someone needing affection.

4. How can you tell if you have given too much affection?

This is a similar activity and requires the child to read the non-verbal signs of someone feeling uncomfortable, embarrassed or annoyed when he or she is the recipient of too much affection. Role playing and video recording can be used to illustrate the signs.

5. How can you tell if you have given not enough affection?

This is an additional activity to explore subtle non-verbal communication signals. Role play and additional resources may also be used.

6. What are the three most important things you have learned about affection?

This is an opportunity to share important new knowledge.

7. Complete the post-programme assessments

This is to record changes in abilities and knowledge using the child's responses to the three stories used in the assessment in the first session too: 'A Walk in the Forest', 'Returning Home from School' and 'A Friend Feeling Sad' (see Appendix 1). The number and type of responses for the child can be compared between the start and end of the programme. This can confirm an increase in the understanding of the value of affection. Parents are also requested to complete the three affection questionnaires at the end of the programme. The child can also be asked which aspects of the programme he or she found especially enjoyable, informative or difficult, and how the programme could be improved.

8. Express affection to someone in the group with a compliment or gesture such as a hug

This is a closing activity when the programme is in a group format to express appreciation and affection for all participants and presenters.

9. Receive your certificate of knowledge!

A certificate of knowledge, signed by the presenters, is awarded to the child.

PART 3

Sessions

Readers have permission to photocopy all worksheets marked with a ✓ for personal use. They are also available to download from www.jkp.com/catalogue/book/9781849054126/resources.

SESSION 1

INTRODUCTION TO THE PROGRAMME
EXPLORING FEELINGS OF AFFECTION

Initial assessment through stories

Read the 'A Walk In the Forest', 'Returning Home from School' and 'A Friend Feeling Sad' stories from Appendix 1 and complete the related activities.

✓

1. The activities and experiences that you like

We all have activities and experiences that we like.

Think of up to ten activities or experiences you like and write them in the spaces below.

Activity or experience	How much you enjoy the activity or experience
_____	_____
_____	_____
_____	_____
_____	_____
_____	_____
_____	_____
_____	_____
_____	_____
_____	_____
_____	_____

Some activities and experiences we like very much, others just a little.

Imagine a scale from 1–100.

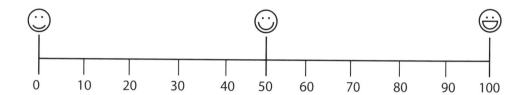

1–10 represents something we like just a little bit.

90–100 represents something we really like a lot.

Next to each activity or experience write the number from 0 to 100 for how much you like each one.

You can choose any number in between, depending on how much you like the activity.

Think carefully before you choose the number.

The person who is helping you will then write down each activity or experience on a yellow 'Post It', and draw a feeling thermometer that measures how strong the feeling is from 0 to 100. You can then stick each 'Post It' at the position on the thermometer that measures how much you like that activity or experience.

We can then look at the thermometer of each of the children in the group today and see if you share any of the same activities, experiences and intensity of feeling.

2. People whom you like or love

Make a list of ten people who you like or love and write each name in the spaces under the word 'Person'.

The person can be someone from your family or a hero from a film, television programme or book.

Person	How much you like that person
_____	_____
_____	_____
_____	_____
_____	_____
_____	_____
_____	_____
_____	_____
_____	_____
_____	_____

Some people we know we like or love very much, other people we like or love just a little.

Imagine a scale from 1–100.

1–10 represents someone we like just a little bit.

90–100 represents someone we love a lot.

Next to each activity or experience write the number from 0 to 100 for how much you like or love each person.

You can choose any number in between, depending on how much you like or love the person.

Liking someone may be measured from 0 to 50, and loving someone from 50 to 100.

Think carefully before you choose the number.

The person who is helping you will write down the name of each person on a yellow 'Post It' and draw another feeling thermometer that measures how strong the feeling of liking or loving that person is from 0 to 100. You can then stick each 'Post It' at the position on the thermometer that measures how much you like or love that person.

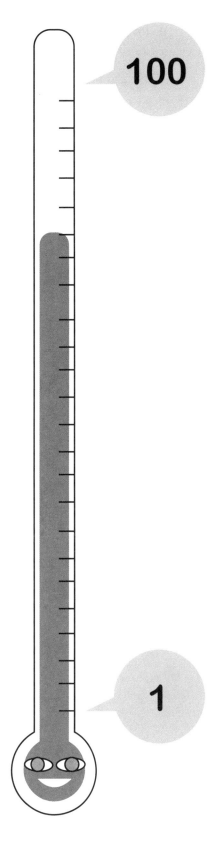

3. How do those people express that they like you or love you?

List all the ways you can think of that people show you how much they like you or love you.

_____

_____

_____

_____

_____

_____

_____

_____

_____

_____

4. How we feel, think and behave when someone likes or loves us

List some of the good things about being liked or loved.

How does being liked or loved affect our feelings, thoughts and abilities?

For example:

When someone likes or loves me, I feel…

_____

_____

_____

_____

_____

✓

When someone likes or loves me, I think…

_____

_____

_____

_____

_____

When someone likes or loves me, I am able to…

_____

_____

_____

_____

_____

✓

5. What would life be like without being liked or loved?

_____

_____

_____

_____

_____

_____

_____

_____

6. List some of the things that are not so
nice about being liked or loved

_____

_____

_____

_____

_____

_____

_____

_____

7. Project: Collect pictures of expressing affection

Find, cut out and save pictures or drawings of people your age expressing that they like or love someone. You might find some pictures in magazines, in clip art on your computer, or on the internet. You will need to collect about 10 to 20 pictures. Keep the pictures in a large envelope and bring the envelope and pictures with you to the next session.

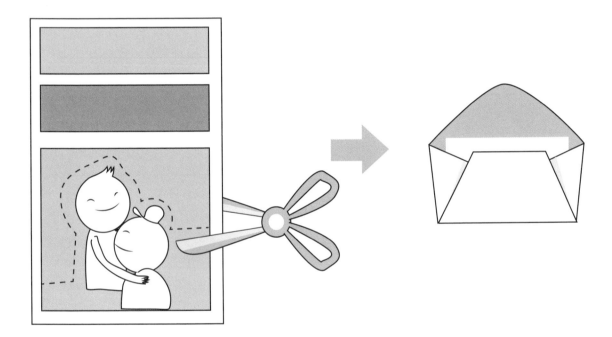

8. Project: Family affection

Sometimes you might find it difficult to express your feelings of love towards your family.

Get your family to think of (and write down) some of those situations where they would expect you to express that you like them or love them, but that you find difficult.

_____

_____

_____

_____

_____

_____

_____

_____

_____

_____

9. Project: Social Story™

Ask your family to help you to write a Social Story™ about how liking or loving someone can affect your feelings, thoughts and abilities, using some of the ideas from today's session.

_____

_____

_____

_____

_____

_____

_____

_____

_____

_____

SESSION 2

BEGINNING TO RECOGNIZE AND EXPRESS AFFECTION

Review of Session 1

Last time we explored some interesting topics: activities and experiences that you like; people who you like; and how we express affection. Let's do a quick quiz to see how much you can remember.

Name one person who you like. How much do you like them (1–50)?

_____

Name one person who you love. How much do you love them (50–100)?

_____

How does that person express their love for you?

_____

_____

✓

How does that make you feel?

_____

_____

What else did you learn from the last session?

_____

_____

1. A Social Story™ about how liking or loving someone can affect your feelings, thoughts and abilities

Include the Social Story™ you have been given here.

✓

2. Using the like and love thermometer to explore pictures of liking and loving

Now you will need the envelope with all the pictures of affection that you collected over the past week.

On the wall there is a 'thermometer' marked from 0–100. On the 'thermometer'…

1–10 represents 'I like the person a little bit.'

Under 50 shows 'I like the person.'

Over 50 shows 'I love the person.'

90–100 represents 'I love the person a lot.'

For each of the pictures that you have collected think about how much loving or liking is being expressed in the picture.

Place the picture on the thermometer where you think it should go.

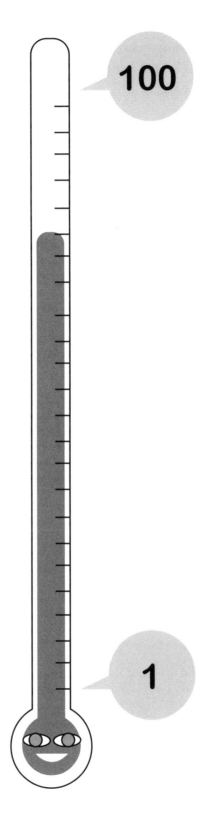

✓

3. What can you say and do to show that you like someone?

The person working with you will write down all things you can say or do to show that you like someone. Use the scale from 1–50 to say how much liking is expressed by each action or statement.

Things to say or do to show that you like the person	**How much liking does this show? (1–50)**
_____	_____
_____	_____
_____	_____
_____	_____
_____	_____
_____	_____

4. What can you say and do to show that you love someone?

The person working with you will write down all the things you can say or do to show that you love someone. Use the scale from 50–100 to say how much loving is expressed by each action or statement.

Things to say or do to show that you love the person	How much loving does this show? (50–100)
_____	_____
_____	_____
_____	_____
_____	_____
_____	_____
_____	_____
_____	_____

5. Project: Use the ideas at home to express liking or loving a member of the family

Sometimes you might find it difficult to express your feelings of love towards your family.

Last week your family thought of (and wrote down) a situation where they would expect you to express that you like them or love them, but that you find difficult.

What was that situation?

_____

_____

_____

_____

_____

_____

Your project is to use some of the ideas from today's session to express liking or loving to a member of your family this week.

When will you express affection?

_____

_____

_____

_____

What type of affection will you express?

_____

_____

_____

_____

✓

Session 3

Giving and receiving compliments

Review of Session 2

We are really exploring affection deeply now.

Last time we placed our liking and loving pictures on the feeling thermometer.

We then wrote down things you can do or say to show that you like or love someone and how much liking or loving is expressed for each action or statement.

1. Review the project from Session 2

Your family thought of (and wrote down) a situation where someone would expect you to express that you like them or love them, but that you find difficult.

Who was the person?

_____

_____

What was that situation?

_____

_____

✓

Your project was to express liking or loving a member of your family in the last week, using some of the ideas you discovered in Session 2.

When did you express affection?

_____

_____

_____

_____

What type of affection did you express?

_____

_____

_____

_____

What did that person say and how did that person feel when you expressed your affection?

_____

_____

_____

_____

How did you feel when you expressed affection?

_____

_____

_____

_____

2. Why do we give compliments?

A compliment is when we say something nice about someone.

Compliments express feelings or thoughts of:

- admiration

- reassurance

- friendship

- encouragement

- liking or loving someone.

When we give a compliment to someone it means we:

_____

_____

_____

_____

3. Compliments for specific people

Write a compliment for a friend that expresses:

admiration _____

_____

reassurance _____

_____

friendship _____

_____

encouragement _____

_____

liking that person _____

_____

✓

Write a compliment for your brother or sister (if you have one) that expresses:

admiration _____

_____

reassurance _____

_____

encouragement _____

_____

loving that person _____

_____

My sister is the best

Write a compliment for your mother or father that expresses:

admiration _____

_____

reassurance _____

_____

encouragement _____

_____

loving that person _____

_____

4. Types of compliment

A compliment can be about a person's:

- abilities
- appearance
- personality.

Write a compliment that you could give your friend about his or her:

abilities _____

_____

appearance _____

_____

personality _____

_____

Write a compliment that you could give your father or mother about his or her:

abilities _____

_____

appearance _____

_____

personality _____

_____

5. How often should you give someone a compliment?

Suggest how many times a day or week you should give a compliment to a:

	Times a day	Times a week
classmate	_____	_____
friend	_____	_____
brother or sister	_____	_____
mother or father	_____	_____

6. How do you reply to a compliment?

When you hear a compliment about you, you can express:

- appreciation
- agreement.

Thank you

Think of some examples of:

appreciation _____

_____

_____

_____

agreement _____

_____

_____

_____

✓

7. Practise giving and receiving compliments

Think of a compliment you could give someone for his or her abilities, appearance or personality.

Actually say that compliment to the person.

How did that person feel when you said the compliment?

_____

_____

_____

_____

_____

How did *you* feel when they expressed their appreciation?

_____

_____

_____

_____

8. Could a compliment be embarrassing?

Sometimes a compliment could be embarrassing to the person who hears it. Can you think of a compliment that could be embarrassing, and why, if it was to a...

classmate _____

_____

_____

friend _____

_____

_____

brother or sister _____

_____

_____

mother or father _____

_____

_____

9. Project: Create a compliment diary

Keep a diary of compliments that you receive and give each day.

✓

THE REASONS WE EXPRESS LIKE OR LOVE THROUGH AFFECTIONATE WORDS AND GESTURES

Review of Session 3

Last time we learned about giving and receiving compliments. Let's see how much you can remember.

Can you think of a compliment for a friend?

_____

_____

Can you think of a compliment for your mum or dad?

_____

_____

What else did you learn from the last session?

_____

_____

1. Review the compliment diary project from Session 3

Over the past week, you kept a diary of compliments that you received and gave each day.

What compliments did you receive?

_____

_____

_____

_____

_____

_____

Who were the compliments from?

_____

_____

_____

_____

How did you feel when you received the compliments?

_____

_____

_____

_____

✓

What compliments did you give?

_____

_____

_____

_____

Who did you give them to?

_____

_____

_____

_____

How did you feel when you gave these compliments?

_____

_____

_____

_____

2. Why do we give affection?

Sometimes the reason a person gives affection can be puzzling.

Why do you think people give each other affection? See how many reasons you can think of, then share them with the group.

_____

_____

_____

_____

_____

_____

_____

_____

_____

_____

_____

_____

3. What would happen if nobody showed you that they liked or loved you?

Draw a picture of your face here…

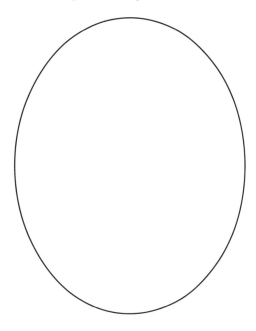

How would you feel?

_____

_____

What would you say?

_____

_____

What would you do?

_____

_____

✔

4. What would happen if you stopped showing your friends that you liked them?

Draw a picture of your friend's face here...

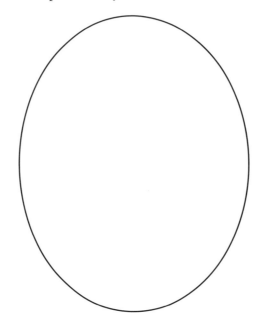

How would he or she feel?

_____

_____

What could you say to help him or her feel better?

_____

_____

What could you do to help him or her feel better?

_____

_____

5. If you did not get enough affection, how could you make yourself feel better?

Things I could do to cheer myself up:

_____

_____

_____

_____

_____

_____

_____

_____

6. How do you feel when...?

Circle the number that measures how you feel when...

(a) Your mum gives you a kiss on the cheek

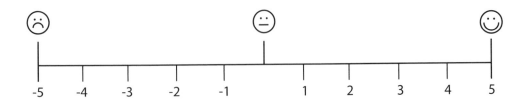

(b) A friend puts his or her arm around your shoulders

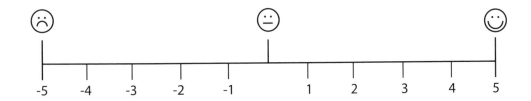

(c) Your mum or dad says, 'I love you'

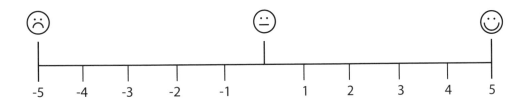

(d) A friend says, 'Well done'

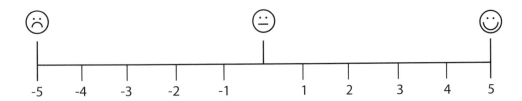

(e) Your dad gives you a quick hug

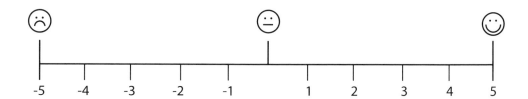

(f) Your mum says you have nice eyes

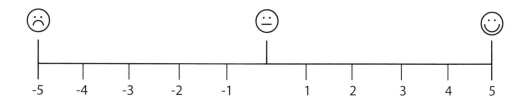

(g) Your mum wants to hold your hand

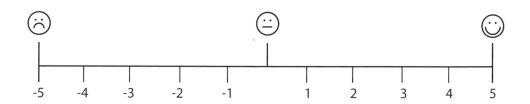

(h) A friend says, 'You are a great friend'

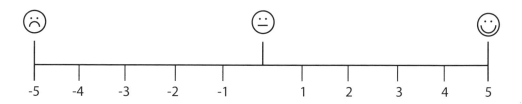

✓

7. Project: Complete a diary of receiving and giving affection

We have a diary for you and your parent or carer to complete over the next week that provides a record of when you expressed and received affection and some examples of the type of affection.

Your name: _____

Please place a ✔ in the box when you have expressed each type of affection.

See if you can express each type of affection at least twice a day.

TYPES OF AFFECTION	WEDNESDAY	THURSDAY	FRIDAY	SATURDAY	SUNDAY	MONDAY	TUESDAY
1. Listen	☐ ☐ ☐	☐ ☐ ☐	☐ ☐ ☐	☐ ☐ ☐	☐ ☐ ☐	☐ ☐ ☐	☐ ☐ ☐
2. Spend fun time with the person	☐ ☐ ☐	☐ ☐ ☐	☐ ☐ ☐	☐ ☐ ☐	☐ ☐ ☐	☐ ☐ ☐	☐ ☐ ☐
3. Do something helpful for the person	☐ ☐ ☐	☐ ☐ ☐	☐ ☐ ☐	☐ ☐ ☐	☐ ☐ ☐	☐ ☐ ☐	☐ ☐ ☐
4. Say 'I love you'	☐ ☐ ☐	☐ ☐ ☐	☐ ☐ ☐	☐ ☐ ☐	☐ ☐ ☐	☐ ☐ ☐	☐ ☐ ☐
5. Kiss or hug the person	☐ ☐ ☐	☐ ☐ ☐	☐ ☐ ☐	☐ ☐ ☐	☐ ☐ ☐	☐ ☐ ☐	☐ ☐ ☐
6. Give the person a compliment	☐ ☐ ☐	☐ ☐ ☐	☐ ☐ ☐	☐ ☐ ☐	☐ ☐ ☐	☐ ☐ ☐	☐ ☐ ☐

Your name: _____

In the spaces provided, briefly record the situations in which you received each of the different types of affection, and who showed them to you.

TYPES OF AFFECTION	WEDNESDAY	THURSDAY	FRIDAY	SATURDAY	SUNDAY	MONDAY	TUESDAY
1. Listen							
2. Spend fun time with the person							
3. Do something helpful for the person							
4. Say 'I love you'							
5. Kiss or hug the person							
6. Give the person a compliment							

Session 5

Developing our skills at expressing affection

Review of Session 4

Last time we explored reasons why we express feelings of like or love by words and gestures of affection. Can you remember some of the feelings you have when someone is affectionate to you?

_____

_____

_____

_____

_____

_____

_____

What could happen if you did not show affection to a friend or someone in your family?

_____

_____

_____

_____

_____

_____

1. Review the diary of receiving and giving affection from Session 4

Review, share and discuss the information and experiences recorded in your diary of receiving and giving affection.

Consider these questions:

Did you enjoy expressing affection?

_____

Which types? To whom?

_____

_____

Did you enjoy receiving affection?

_____

Which types? By whom?

_____

_____

Did you express too much or too little affection?

_____

How did you know?

_____

_____

✓

Did you receive enough affection?

_____

Are there any situations in which you do not like to give or receive affection? What are they?

_____

2. Different types of affection in different situations

The matching game

Here is a list of situations and a list of different types of affection. See if you can match the best type of affection for the situation by drawing a line between the situation and the type of affection.

Situation	Type of affection
Your dad or carer is trying to talk to someone on the phone and doing the washing-up at the same time.	Pat on the head
Your mum or carer smiles at you.	Hand shake
It is bedtime and time to say 'good night' to your parent or carer.	Close, long hug
It is time to go to school and time to say 'goodbye' to your parent or carer.	Quick kiss on the cheek
Your friend hits a difficult-to-hit ball in a tennis game.	Hold hands
Your parent or carer says, 'I love you.'	Kiss on the lips
A stranger says, 'Hello' and holds out their hand.	Saying, 'You are my best friend'
The postman comes to your house.	Saying, 'I love you'
Your parent or carer is crying.	Arm around the shoulders
Your friend has fallen off his or her bike and has hurt himself.	Quick hug
Your aunt has come to visit and it is time to say 'Hello' to her.	Saying, 'You have nice eyes'
You see someone you do not know.	Saying, 'Well done!'
Your mum or carer cooks you your favourite meal.	Pat on the back
Your friend gives you a pat on the back.	Saying, 'Thank you'
Your friend gives you a nice present.	Saying, 'I like the way you did that'

3. How can you tell if someone needs affection?

What are the signs that someone needs affection? Think of the person's facial expression, body language, words and tone of voice, the situation and what you know about that person. Think of the signs you would notice in different situations.

Facial expression _____

_____

Body language _____

_____

Words _____

_____

Tone of voice _____

_____

The situation _____

_____

What you know about the person _____

_____

See if you can you have a go expressing those signs yourself and noticing them in the facial expression, body language and tone of voice of the person you are working with.

4. How can you tell if you have given *too much* affection?

What are the signs in someone's facial expression, body language and words?

Facial expression _____

_____

Body language _____

_____

Words _____

_____

How will that person feel? _____

_____

5. How can you tell if you have given *not enough* affection?

What are the signs in someone's facial expression, body language and words?

Facial expression _____

_____

Body language _____

_____

Words _____

_____

How will that person feel? _____

_____

6. What are the three most important things
you have learned about affection?

1. _____

   _____

2. _____

   _____

3. _____

   _____

7. Complete the post-programme assessments

Complete the 'A Walk in the Forest', 'Returning Home from School' and 'A Friend Feeling Sad' activities from Session 1 again. What changes can you see in your understanding of affection since the beginning of the programme?

_____

_____

_____

_____

_____

_____

_____

_____

_____

✓

8. Express affection to someone in the group with a compliment or gesture such as a hug

9. Receive your certificate of knowledge!

REFERENCES

Andrews, L., Attwood, T. and Sofronoff, K. (under review) 'Increasing the appropriate demonstration of affectionate behaviour in children with Asperger syndrome: A randomized controlled trial.' *Research in Autism Spectrum Disorders.*

Attwood, T. and Garnett, M. (2013) *From Like to Love for Young People with Asperger's Syndrome (Autism Spectrum Disorder): Learning How to Express and Enjoy Affection with Family and Friends.* London: Jessica Kingsley Publishers.

Grandin, T. and Barron, S. (2005) *Unwritten Rules of Social Relationships.* Arlington, TX: Future Horizons.

Sofronoff, K., Eloff, J., Sheffield, J. and Attwood, T. (2011) 'Increasing the understanding and demonstration of appropriate affection in children with Asperger syndrome: A pilot trial.' *Autism Research and Treatment,* volume 2011, doi:10.1155/2011/214317.

Sofronoff, K., Lee, J., Sheffield, J. and Attwood, T. (in press) 'The construction and evaluation of three measures of affectionate behaviour for children with Asperger's syndrome.' *Autism.*

Recommended resources

CAT-kit by Kirsten Callesen, Annette Moller-Nielsen and Tony Attwood published in 2008 by Future Horizons, Arlington, Texas.

The New Social Story Book by Carol Gray published in 2010 by Future Horizons, Arlington, Texas.

Mind Reading: The Interactive Guide to Emotions DVD distributed by Jessica Kingsley Publishers, London. The programme uses an interactive DVD and can be used with children from age six to adults. More information available from www.jkp.com.

✓

APPENDIX 1
STORIES USED IN THE ASSESSMENT PROGRAMME

A Walk in the Forest

Imagine it is early morning and you are walking along a path in a forest. As you come to the middle of the forest, you notice that several trees have fallen to the ground. You are curious, as you know that there have been no high winds recently that would explain why the trees have come down. As you climb over the tree trunks, you see that in the middle of the fallen trees there is what looks like a small space ship.

As you carefully approach it, there is a strange noise and an opening appears at the front of the space ship. Out of the opening comes a glowing object, about the size and shape of a tennis ball. The glowing shape hovers just above you, and then slowly descends to become level with your eyes. Suddenly it disappears and there in front of you is someone who looks exactly like you.

The person who looks exactly the same as you starts to speak, with a voice the same as yours. This duplicate 'you' explains that it is an alien that has crashed on planet earth while observing humans. It explains that the space ship will be repaired in a few hours, but before leaving, the alien has a very important question to ask you about humans.

The alien has observed that humans seem to need to communicate that they like or love one another, and that they do this by saying nice things to each other and touching one another. It has observed that this behaviour seems to happen particularly between friends and family members. The alien is curious as to why humans do this.

Can you explain to the alien why humans are affectionate with each other?

_____

_____

_____

_____

The alien now understands and gives you a special present. What present could the alien give you?

_____

_____

_____

_____

_____

Returning Home from School

Imagine you have just returned home from school. You walk into the kitchen to let your mother know that you are home. You see that she is sitting at the kitchen table with her back to you. As you say 'Hi', she turns round and you notice that she is crying.

What would you do or say first?

_____

_____

_____

_____

_____

What could you do or say to make her feel better?

_____

_____

_____

_____

_____

_____

A Friend Feeling Sad

Imagine you have arrived at school, just before your friend. As your friend enters the school grounds, you notice your friend looks very sad. Your friend explains that early that morning, his or her dog escaped from home, ran across a road, was hit by a car, and died.

What could you do or say to make your friend feel better?

_____

_____

_____

_____

_____

_____

APPENDIX 2
AFFECTION QUESTIONNAIRES

From Sofronoff, Lee, Sheffield and Attwood (in press).

THE AFFECTION FOR OTHERS QUESTIONNAIRE (AOQ)

The questions below are all to do with the types of affection your child (aged between 5 years and 13 years old) with autism spectrum disorder shows *others*. This means the affection that he or she shows to people outside of his or her immediate family such as: school teachers, classmates, family friends, shopkeepers and strangers. Please fill this out even if your child has very few difficulties expressing affection for others.

There are two components to each question:

1. How appropriately does your child show others that form of affection?

Consider how **appropriately** your child shows affection to **others** by rating this on a seven-point scale, from 'never' to 'always'.

a) How appropriate is the amount of affection he or she shows others?

Consider how appropriate you find the **amount** of affection your child shows to **others** by giving a rating on the seven-point scale.

Please see the example below:

1. Is your child able to say 'hello' to others in an appropriate manner?

1	2	3	4	5	6	7
Never appropriate			Sometimes			Always appropriate

For example, if you rated this as a '1' your child would never say 'hello' in an appropriate manner, and may shout it at people or ignore people when a 'hello' would be appropriate.

a) What do you think of the amount he/she does this?

1	2	3	4	5	6	7
Not enough			About right			Too much

For example, if you rated this as a '1' it would mean that you consider your child is rarely appropriate when saying 'hello' to others because he or she does not do it enough. Alternatively you may rate it as a '6' or '7' if the reason that your child was not able to say 'hello' in an appropriate manner was because he or she did it too frequently.

There are 20 questions in this section.

The first 8 questions are about your child GIVING affection to **others**. Examples of 'others' are: school teachers, classmates, family friends, shopkeepers, and strangers.

GIVING VERBAL AFFECTION

1. Is your child able to say 'I love you/I like you' to others appropriately (e.g. classmates or family friends)?

1 Never appropriate	2	3	4 Sometimes	5	6	7 Always appropriate

a) What do you think of the amount he/she does this?

1 Not enough	2	3	4 About right	5	6	7 Too much

2. Is your child able to say something to others about how important the relationship between them is appropriately?

1 Never appropriate	2	3	4 Sometimes	5	6	7 Always appropriate

a) What do you think of the amount he/she does this?

1 Not enough	2	3	4 About right	5	6	7 Too much

3. Is your child able to compliment others in an appropriate way?

1 Never appropriate	2	3	4 Sometimes	5	6	7 Always appropriate

a) What do you think of the amount he/she does this?

1 Not enough	2	3	4 About right	5	6	7 Too much

4. Is your child able to speak to others in an appropriately friendly manner?

1 Never appropriate	2	3	4 Sometimes	5	6	7 Always appropriate

a) What do you think of the amount he/she does this?

1 Not enough	2	3	4 About right	5	6	7 Too much

GIVING PHYSICAL AFFECTION

5. Is your child able to hug others appropriately?

1 Never appropriate	2	3	4 Sometimes	5	6	7 Always appropriate

a) What do you think of the amount he/she does this?

1 Not enough	2	3	4 About right	5	6	7 Too much

6. Is your child able to hold others' hands appropriately when he/she needs to (e.g. a school teacher)?

1 Never appropriate	2	3	4 Sometimes	5	6	7 Always appropriate

a) What do you think of the amount he/she does this?

1 Not enough	2	3	4 About right	5	6	7 Too much

7. Is your child able to put his/her arm around the shoulder of others appropriately (e.g. classmates)?

1 Never appropriate	2	3	4 Sometimes	5	6	7 Always appropriate

a) What do you think of the amount he/she does this?

1 Not enough	2	3	4 About right	5	6	7 Too much

8. Is your child able to physically acknowledge others appropriately, by giving them a touch on the arm, pat on the back, or similar?

1 Never appropriate	2	3	4 Sometimes	5	6	7 Always appropriate

a) What do you think of the amount he/she does this?

1 Not enough	2	3	4 About right	5	6	7 Too much

The next 8 questions are about your child accepting and RECEIVING affection from **others**.

RECEIVING VERBAL AFFECTION

9. Is your child able to respond appropriately to others saying 'I like you/I love you' to him/her (e.g. classmates)?

1 Never appropriate	2	3	4 Sometimes	5	6	7 Always appropriate

a) What do you think of the amount he/she does this?

1 Not enough	2	3	4 About right	5	6	7 Too much

10. Is your child able to respond to compliments from others?

	1 Never appropriate	2	3	4 Sometimes	5	6	7 Always appropriate

a) What do you think of the amount he/she does this?

	1 Not enough	2	3	4 About right	5	6	7 Too much

11. Is your child able to accept thanks or praise from others appropriately?

	1 Never appropriate	2	3	4 Sometimes	5	6	7 Always appropriate

a) What do you think of the amount he/she does this?

	1 Not enough	2	3	4 About right	5	6	7 Too much

12. Is your child able to speak in an appropriately friendly manner back to others when he/she is included in a conversation?

	1 Never appropriate	2	3	4 Sometimes	5	6	7 Always appropriate

a) What do you think of the amount he/she does this?

	1 Not enough	2	3	4 About right	5	6	7 Too much

RECEIVING PHYSICAL AFFECTION

13. Is your child able to receive a hug from others appropriately (e.g. classmates or family friends)?

1 Never appropriate	2	3	4 Sometimes	5	6	7 Always appropriate

a) What do you think of the amount he/she does this?

1 Not enough	2	3	4 About right	5	6	7 Too much

14. Is your child able to respond to a kiss from others appropriately (e.g. family friend)?

1 Never appropriate	2	3	4 Sometimes	5	6	7 Always appropriate

a) What do you think of the amount he/she does this?

1 Not enough	2	3	4 About right	5	6	7 Too much

15. Is your child able to react appropriately when others touch him/her (e.g. classmates)?

1 Never appropriate	2	3	4 Sometimes	5	6	7 Always appropriate

a) What do you think of the amount he/she does this?

1 Not enough	2	3	4 About right	5	6	7 Too much

16. Is your child able to react appropriately when others give him/her a pat on the back (e.g. classmates)?

1 Never appropriate	2	3	4 Sometimes	5	6	7 Always appropriate

a) What do you think of the amount he/she does this?

1 Not enough	2	3	4 About right	5	6	7 Too much

The final 4 questions are about your child's ability to understand and share emotions with **others**.

COMMUNICATION OF EMPATHY

17. Is your child able to laugh appropriately with others?

1 Never appropriate	2	3	4 Sometimes	5	6	7 Always appropriate

a) What do you think of the amount he/she does this?

1 Not enough	2	3	4 About right	5	6	7 Too much

18. Is your child able to show an appropriate level of interest in the actions and feelings of others?

1 Never appropriate	2	3	4 Sometimes	5	6	7 Always appropriate

a) What do you think of the amount he/she does this?

1 Not enough	2	3	4 About right	5	6	7 Too much

19. Is your child able to be appropriately helpful to others?

1 Never appropriate	2	3	4 Sometimes	5	6	7 Always appropriate

a) What do you think of the amount he/she does this?

1 Not enough	2	3	4 About right	5	6	7 Too much

20. Is your child able to smile at others appropriately?

1 Never appropriate	2	3	4 Sometimes	5	6	7 Always appropriate

a) What do you think of the amount he/she does this?

1 Not enough	2	3	4 About right	5	6	7 Too much

THE AFFECTION FOR YOU QUESTIONNAIRE (AYQ)

The next questions are all to do with the types of affection your child (aged between 5 years and 13 years old) with autism spectrum disorder shows *you*. Please fill these questions out even if your child does not have any difficulty expressing affection to you.

There are two components to each question:

1. How often does your child show you that form of affection?

Consider how **often** your child shows affection to **you** by rating this on a seven-point scale, from 'never' to 'twice a day or more'.

a) How appropriate is the amount of affection he or she shows you?

Consider the **amount** of affection your child shows **you** by giving a rating on the seven-point scale.

Please see the example below:

	1	2	3	4	5	6	7
1. How often does he/she say 'hello' to you?	Never	Yearly	Monthly	2 x week	1 x week	1 x day	2 x day or more

For example, if you rated this as a '6' your child would say 'hello' to you once a day on average.

	1	2	3	4	5	6	7
a) What do you think of the amount they say this?	Not enough			About right			Too much

For example, if you rated this as a '4' it would mean that you consider your child saying 'hello' to you once a day to be about the 'right' amount.

There are 19 questions in this section.

The first 9 questions are about your child GIVING affection to **you.** Please consider how often he/she does this as well as how satisfied you are with this amount.

GIVING VERBAL AFFECTION

1. How often does he/she say 'I love you' to *you?*

1	2	3	4	5	6	7
Never	Yearly	Monthly	2 x week	1 x week	1 x day	2 x day or more

a) What do you think of the amount he/she does this?

1	2	3	4	5	6	7
Not enough			About right			Too much

2. How often does he/she say something to *you* about how important your relationship is to him/her?

1	2	3	4	5	6	7
Never	Yearly	Monthly	2 x week	1 x week	1 x day	2 x day or more

a) What do you think of the amount he/she does this?

1	2	3	4	5	6	7
Not enough			About right			Too much

3. How often does he/she thank *you?*

1	2	3	4	5	6	7
Never	Yearly	Monthly	2 x week	1 x week	1 x day	2 x day or more

a) What do you think of the amount he/she does this?

1	2	3	4	5	6	7
Not enough			About right			Too much

		1 Never	2 Yearly	3 Monthly	4 2 x week	5 1 x week	6 1 x day	7 2 x day or more
4.	How often does he/she speak to *you* in a friendly manner?							
		1 Not enough	2	3	4 About right	5	6	7 Too much
a)	What do you think of the amount he/she does this?							

GIVING PHYSICAL AFFECTION

		1 Never	2 Yearly	3 Monthly	4 2 x week	5 1 x week	6 1 x day	7 2 x day or more
5.	How often does he/she come up and hug *you*?							
		1 Not enough	2	3	4 About right	5	6	7 Too much
a)	What do you think of the amount he/she does this?							

		1 Never	2 Yearly	3 Monthly	4 2 x week	5 1 x week	6 1 x day	7 2 x day or more
6.	How often does he/she want to hold *your* hand?							
		1 Not enough	2	3	4 About right	5	6	7 Too much
a)	What do you think of the amount he/she does this?							

7. How often does he/she want to sit close to *you*?

1	2	3	4	5	6	7
Never	Yearly	Monthly	2 x week	1 x week	1 x day	2 x day or more

a) What do you think of the amount he/she does this?

1	2	3	4	5	6	7
Not enough			About right			Too much

8. How often does he/she put his/her arm around *your* shoulder, around your waist, or around your legs?

1	2	3	4	5	6	7
Never	Yearly	Monthly	2 x week	1 x week	1 x day	2 x day or more

a) What do you think of the amount he/she does this?

1	2	3	4	5	6	7
Not enough			About right			Too much

9. How often does he/she acknowledge *your* presence by touching you in some way, e.g. a pat on the back or arm, a touch on the hand, or similar?

1	2	3	4	5	6	7
Never	Yearly	Monthly	2 x week	1 x week	1 x day	2 x day or more

a) What do you think of the amount he/she does this?

1	2	3	4	5	6	7
Not enough			About right			Too much

The next 6 questions are about your child accepting and RECEIVING affection from **you**.

RECEIVING VERBAL AFFECTION

10. How often does he/she say 'I love you' back to *you*?

1 Never	2 Yearly	3 Monthly	4 2 x week	5 1 x week	6 1 x day	7 2 x day or more

a) What do you think of the amount he/she does this?

1 Not enough	2	3	4 About right	5	6	7 Too much

11. How often does he/she respond with pleasure to *you* using a pet name or term of endearment to refer to him/her?

1 Never	2 Yearly	3 Monthly	4 2 x week	5 1 x week	6 1 x day	7 2 x day or more

a) What do you think of the amount he/she does this?

1 Not enough	2	3	4 About right	5	6	7 Too much

12. How often does he/she speak in a friendly manner back to *you*?

1 Never	2 Yearly	3 Monthly	4 2 x week	5 1 x week	6 1 x day	7 2 x day or more

a) What do you think of the amount she/she does this?

1 Not enough	2	3	4 About right	5	6	7 Too much

RECEIVING PHYSICAL AFFECTION

13. How often does he/she enjoy it when *you* hug him/her?

1	2	3	4	5	6	7
Never	Yearly	Monthly	2 x week	1 x week	1 x day	2 x day or more

a) What do you think of the amount he/she does this?

1	2	3	4	5	6	7
Not enough			About right			Too much

14. How often does he/she enjoy it when *you* kiss him/her?

1	2	3	4	5	6	7
Never	Yearly	Monthly	2 x week	1 x week	1 x day	2 x day or more

a) What do you think of the amount he/she does this?

1	2	3	4	5	6	7
Not enough			About right			Too much

15. How often does he/she hold hands with you when *you* ask him/her to?

1	2	3	4	5	6	7
Never	Yearly	Monthly	2 x week	1 x week	1 x day	2 x day or more

a) What do you think of the amount he/she does this?

1	2	3	4	5	6	7
Not enough			About right			Too much

The final 4 questions are about your child's ability to understand and share emotions with **you**.

COMMUNICATION OF EMPATHY

		1 Never	2 Yearly	3 Monthly	4 2 x week	5 1 x week	6 1 x day	7 2 x day or more
16.	How often does he/she laugh with *you?*							
a)	What do you think of the amount he/she does this?	1 Not enough	2	3	4 About right	5	6	7 Too much
17.	How often does he/she show an interest in what *you* are doing or feeling?	1 Never	2 Yearly	3 Monthly	4 2 x week	5 1 x week	6 1 x day	7 2 x day or more
a)	What do you think of the amount he/she does this?	1 Not enough	2	3	4 About right	5	6	7 Too much

18. How often is he/she helpful when *you* need it?

1	2	3	4	5	6	7
Never	Yearly	Monthly	2 x week	1 x week	1 x day	2 x day or more

a) What do you think of the amount he/she does this?

1	2	3	4	5	6	7
Not enough			About right			Too much

19. How often does he/she smile at *you* with happiness?

1	2	3	4	5	6	7
Never	Yearly	Monthly	2 x week	1 x week	1 x day	2 x day or more

a) What do you think of the amount he/she does this?

1	2	3	4	5	6	7
Not enough			About right			Too much

THE GENERAL AFFECTION QUESTIONNAIRE (GAQ)

Please answer the following questions about your child by circling a number that shows your level of agreement with the following 12 statements.

---

1. He/she has only a limited number of ways of expressing affection.

1	2	3	4	5	6	7
Strongly disagree						Strongly agree

---

2. He/she shows a lack of affection.

1	2	3	4	5	6	7
Strongly disagree						Strongly agree

---

3. He/she has difficulties initiating affection.

1	2	3	4	5	6	7
Strongly disagree						Strongly agree

---

4. He/she finds it difficult receiving affection from others.

1	2	3	4	5	6	7
Strongly disagree						Strongly agree

---

5. He/she uses inappropriate expressions of affection.

1	2	3	4	5	6	7
Strongly disagree						Strongly agree

6. I have had to spend time teaching him/her about affection.

1	2	3	4	5	6	7
Strongly disagree						Strongly agree

7. There seems to be a difference between his/her physical need for touch and his/her desire to express affection.

1	2	3	4	5	6	7
Strongly disagree						Strongly agree

8. He/she has difficulties with affection and these interfere with school.

1	2	3	4	5	6	7
Strongly disagree						Strongly agree

9. He/she has difficulties with affection that cause problems with his/her siblings.

1	2	3	4	5	6	7
Strongly disagree						Strongly agree

10. He/she has difficulties displaying affection to those outside of our immediate family.

1	2	3	4	5	6	7
Strongly disagree						Strongly agree

11. He/she has quirky or unusual ways of giving or wanting to receive affection.

1	2	3	4	5	6	7
Strongly disagree						Strongly agree

12. He/she has difficulties understanding that certain types and levels of affection are not appropriate to show to everyone (e.g. does not discriminate well between those who it is appropriate to hug/kiss/touch).

1	2	3	4	5	6	7
Strongly disagree						Strongly agree